AMAZON'S NATURE OF THINGS

NORTHWATER

CONSTANTINE ISSIGHOS

Copyright 2012 © Constantine Issighos. Published in Canada. Printed in U.S.A. No part of this book may be reproduced or transmitted in any form or by any means, electronic or mechanical, including photocopying, recording, and/or by any information storage and retrieval system except by a reviewer who may quote brief passages in a review to be printed in a magazine, newspaper, or on the web without written permission in writing from the author/publisher. For information, please contact www.awaqkunabooks.com

NorthWater is an imprint of Awaqkuna Books Inc.

Vol. 4 of THE AMAZON EXPLORATION SERIES:
AMAZON'S NATURE OF THINGS

Library and Archives Canada

ISBN 978-0-9878599-3-8

Library and Archives Canada Cataloguing in Publication

ATTENTION CHILDRENS ASSOCIATIONS, BOOK STORES, PUBLIC OR PRIVATE LIBRARIES: quantity discounts are available on bulk purchases of this book series.

THE AMAZON EXPLORATION SERIES

Children's Books
by
Constantine Issighos

1. Upper Amazon Voyage by River Boat
2. The People of the River
3. The Children of the River
4. Amazon's Nature of Things
5. Echoes of Nature: a Beautiful Wild Habitat
6. The Amazon Rainforest
7. Amazonian Sisterhood
8. Amazon River Wolves
9. Amazonian Landscapes and Sunsets
10. Amazonian Canopy: the Roof of the World's Rainforest
11. Amazonian Tribes: a World of Difference
12. Birds and Butterflies of the Amazon
13. The Great Wonders of the Amazon
14. The Jaguar People
15. The Fresh Water Giants
16. The Call of the Shaman
17. Indigenous Families: Life in Harmony with Nature
18. Amazon in Peril
19. Giant Tarantulas and Centipedes

Look around. We humans share our Earth with a diverse range of plants and animals. Due to this fact, we all depend upon each other for survival. Life is created, shaped and supported by other life forms in a continuous, interdependent pattern that all creatures rely upon for survival. From the smallest organisms to the top carnivores, all have their place in the natural scheme of things. This is the Earth's natural balance. The Amazon River of South America is a primary example. Nutrients are carried along its vast river banks to the network of streams where a diversity of freshwater fish spawn. Birds and jungle animals feed on river fish. Plants and soils store carbon, keeping it from the Earth's atmosphere, where it would contribute to climate change. These natural systems are often taken for granted, without recognizing and appreciating their delicate balance.

By learning more about what we have and why we need to preserve and protect the biodiversity of the Amazon rainforest, we can all work to make sure that we maintain and restore Earth's natural balance, which all life on Earth needs to survive. The Amazon rainforest is the "Mother Jungle," providing 20% of the Earth's oxygen. It is home to some of the last free-roaming animals and its diverse vegetation displays great splendour. It is Nature without human manipulation.

When I travel into the vast interior of the Amazon rainforest, my senses recognize this awesome environment and all of my cells awaken from their urban lethargy. My inner biology readjusts to the rhythms and sounds offered to me by the mighty music of the concert of Life in this Sacred Garden. My mind is slowly cleansed and I begin to clearly hear the sounds of the birds, the freshwater fish and caiman splashing upon the river's surface, the rain and the wind. For the first time in my life, I hear the powerful sound of the approaching rainstorm before it breaks into thunderous rainfall.

When the rain stops, the equatorial sun comes with its life-giving embrace. All living organisms engage in their eternal lifecycle--Birth, Growth and Death--in the "Mother Jungle." My senses connect with all that is around me, and an ancient and immense peace fills my body and mind.

I am in a natural universe of countless reptiles and insects and of unique land and water mammals—primates, felines, tapirs, freshwater giants, Arapaima (Paiche), Black Caiman, Otters, Piranha, Anaconda and Pink and Grey Dolphins; to name just a few. An endless canopy of giant trees shelters medicinal plants and barks used by indigenous tribes.

In the indigenous society, the Amazon Basin comprises both *Sacha* (forest) and *Chacra* (cultivated fields). Nature is simultaneously wild and domesticated a source of knowledge and a principle of fertility. The indigenous culture includes ecological knowledge, agricultural skills, hunting, fishing, and the healing power of medicinal plants. The knowledge and skills are both material and cultural, for they are embedded with cultural meanings that tie together the human and the non-human, the wild and the cultivated.

Indigenous society is egalitarian and important communal decision-making is rooted within the community. Division of labour among men and women is based on the main productive activities. Women are in charge of the family fields. Men also participate in the agricultural activities by lifting heavy loads etc., but men are mainly responsible for hunting, fishing, and gathering medicinal barks and plants which takes them deep into the jungle for many days.

However, the gender roles in food production convey a fundamental gender-based knowledge of the Amazon environment: women are deeply involved in the knowledge of crops-- in the family's *chacra*-- while men, as warriors have the knowledge of hunting and mastering the forest. We must be careful here, for there is not a defined gender border. Most significant variations in ecological knowledge are found between indigenous families, rather than across gender lines. Their communal ecological knowledge is shaped by the climate of the Amazon Basin which, in turn, is strongly dependent on the forest.

In comparison to unforested land, the Amazon Basin forest enhances evapotranspiration through the extraction of moisture deep in the soil by vegetative roots. The giant tree canopy captures a great amount of rainfall which is then re-evaporated back into the atmosphere. This is not the case when compared to deforested land, which holds less water on the surface before runoff and infiltration. The higher roughness of the forested land surface can maintain the flow of moisture to the atmosphere through enhanced turbulence.

From the murky depths of the ancient Maranon River, once hidden deep within the maze of the Amazon Basin, a floating slab of tree roots and solid mud slowly makes its way following the river current. It is a giant chunk taken from the bottom skin of the riverbed, holding thousands of years of geological history. Like a freshly caught prize Arapaima fish, it is floating on the surface for all inhabitants to see.

The great mystery of the prehistoric Amazon forest, with its giant tree columns and green canopy, fills the entire length of the banks of the Amazon River. I stand and stare at the lifeless form of the muddy roots, wondering if hidden deep within its innards is the key that research scientists would need to unlock the mystery of its origins.

I think that somewhere in this grey blob may be preserved pollen grains that tell the story of the pre- historic Amazon, traces of the forest hidden away until now, like footprints that give away a geological event.

The origin of the Amazon is one of the great unknowns of science. In this unknown historical past lies the origin of the biodiversity of the richest ecosystem on Earth. A long prevalent view is of an unchanged Amazonian ecosystem, with its past like its present. Another theory is that in the Ice Age that covered most of America, species gathered in the warm and humid Amazonian ecosystem to avoid the perils of the freezing Ice Age temperatures. Long prevalent were both views; but both have been challenged by botanists and biologists, who imagine an arid and decimated Ice Age Amazon Basin, with pockets of forest existing in a few patches of wetlands. Only after the climate warmed did the surviving plants and animals radiate back out again. Mud and pollen and scientific research have begun to show how this vast green basin was formed and built. Biological and geographical theories are of the utmost importance in understanding the biodiversity of the Amazon, so that young people and adults can read of its past in order to protect its future. By investigating how this green canopy was formed and built, we can predict whether its deforestation can be reversed.

As I was flying from Lima to the jungle city of Iquitos, the rainforest canopy covering the vast Amazon Basin appeared from the air like a uniform green carpet split by the long winding river. Contrary to its appearance, the Amazon River Basin is not uniform. Its canopy is formed by broad leaves of many different kinds of giant trees. This canopy at the topmost layer of the Amazon ecosystem supports more species than any other forested region on Earth.

The rainforest canopy is characterized by a unique massive vegetative structure consisting of several horizontal layers including the upper canopy, with its dense ceiling and branches, the understory, the shrub and the ground level. The average upper canopy is 55 to 100 meters (120 to 280 feet) above the ground level. Below the upper canopy, and penetrated by scattered emergent vines, is the level known as the understory. Scattered parasitic vines choke the giant trees, as the former strive to reach the top canopy or overstory. These parasitic vines form the multiple leaf and branch level known as the understory.

Below the understory, 3 to 8 meters (10 to 25 feet) above ground level is the shrub layer, consisting of shrubby vegetation and tree saplings. The dense vegetation of the upper canopy effectively blocks daylight and in a truly primary equatorial forest there is little jungle-like ground growth to impede movement. Ground level vegetation in a primary forest environment is minimal and consists mainly of vines and tree seedlings.

A unique characteristic of the Amazonian canopy system is the presence of different plants that grow on giant canopy trees. Some of these plants are parasitic; others are not. Unlike the parasitic vines, plants known as *epiphytes* draw no nutrients away from the host, but use the host tree only as support. High up in the overstory, epiphytes are better able to access humidity and the strong tropical light, which they require for growth. They have adapted well to their aerial surroundings, developing various means to collect the nutrients they need from the environment.

An additional plant type of the Amazonian canopy system is the *liana*. It is a wooden vine that begins on the forest floor and makes its way up to the canopy by latching on to canopy trees. This can be deadly for as the liana grows stronger, it squeezes the life out of the host tree. A plant that is truly parasitic is a related type of plant, the hemi-epiphyte, which begins life in the canopy. It also lives off the nutrients of the host tree until it grows long roots that eventually reach the forest floor. Once rooted, the hemi-epiphyte does not have to rely on drawn nutrients from the surrounding canopy, but can access nutrients from the forest floor.

The Amazon Basin forest is a leafy world. An unknown number of plants and animals reside in the canopy level, the large majority of which are specifically adapted to life in this aerial environment. In tropical rainforests, it is calculated that 90% of the resident species live in the canopy. Additional estimates reveal that the tropical rainforests hold 50% of the Earth's species; the canopy of rainforests worldwide may hold as much as 48% of the life on our planet.

CHARACTERISTICS OF THE TROPICAL RAINFOREST

The latest scientific evidence claims that the vast biodiversity of the Amazon Basin is the result of catastrophic geological events. Rather than a stable geological system, the Amazon is in a continual process of change. Such change contributes to the rejuvenation of life in the Amazon. The moderate climate disturbances in the region help account for the splendid biodiversity of the Amazon rainforest.

The Amazon was formed some 15 million years ago, when the Andean mountain corridor of the South America Plate collided with the Nazca Plate in what is now Peru. The rise of the corridor blocked the river and caused the Amazon to become a massive, swampy, freshwater lake, and the once seawater marine life adapted to life in freshwater. For example, dolphins, most closely related to those found in the oceans, can be found today in the freshwater of the Amazon River.

About 10 million years ago, the Amazon's swampy water level dropped, rapidly drained and it became a river. About 7 million years later, the Amazon Basin allowed the settlement of a mass migration of mammal species from Central America.

Although much debated, scientists around the world believe that the main formative factor of today's tropical rainforest was the Ice Age. It caused the Amazon to revert to savanna and mountain forest. The savanna divided patches of rainforest and separated existing species for millennia, long enough to allow genetic modifications. About 6000 years ago, some the plants and animals of the Amazon forest had enough genetic differentiation to be classified as separate species, thus adding to the tremendous diversity of the tropical Amazon rainforest.

Tropical rainforests lie between the Tropic of Cancer and the Tropic of Capricorn. In this geographical region, the sun's rays strike the Earth at a 90-degree angle, resulting in intense solar energy. This steady equatorial daylight, 12 hours a day throughout the year, provides the essential solar energy to power the tropical rainforest by photosynthesis. This ample solar energy keeps the Amazon rainforest hot and humid throughout the year with a temperature range of about 75-95 degrees. Of course, the temperature may vary during the year, but the average daily temperature does not fluctuate more than 0.5 degrees throughout the year.

An important characteristic of the rainforest lies within its name. Intense solar energy produces a precipitation zone of rising air that loses its moisture through frequent heavy rainstorms. I have witnessed heavy rainstorms in the Upper Amazon Basin of Loreto, Peru and I have seen its destructive power on crops and indigenous shelters.

The minimum rainfall may be 2 meters (6.5ft) per year, and in most areas may be over 12 meters (35 feet) of rain per year. In regions where there is year-round rainfall there is not a noticeable wet or dry season. Even during seasonal rainstorms, the periods between rains are not long enough for the ground vegetation to dry out completely. During the months of the dry season, there still is a constant cloud cover which is enough to keep both the air moist and the plants from drying out. Even in apparent dry seasons, rarely is there a month without at least 2.36 cm (6 inches) of rain. The general precipitation, with evenly spread moisture and warmth, allows vegetation to be evergreen. Leaves are maintained throughout the year and are constantly being rejuvenated. Moisture from rainfall and the constant cloud cover and transpiration create intense localized humidity. Each giant canopy tree transpires some 820 litters (205 gallons) of water annually. The humidity of the large rainforests, like the Upper Amazon Region of Peru, contributes to the formation of rain clouds and generates roughly 75 percent of its own rainfall.

INTERDEPENCE OF SPECIES WITHIN THE RAINFOREST ECOSYSTEM

Life in the Amazon is competitive and species have developed a complex interdependent–symbiotic—relationship with other species in order to survive. Interdependence is, therefore, a key characteristic of the rainforest ecosystem. For example, biological interdependency takes many forms in the forest, from species relying on other species for pollination and seed dispersal to predatory/prey symbiotic relationships. These interdependent relationships have been developing for millions of years and form the biological basis for the ecosystem. Honey bees, for example, are dependent on flowers for their nectar and the flowers rely for their pollination on orchid bees. As the bees travel from flower to a flower, pollen carried on their legs is then transferred upon landing to the next host flower.

Each species that disappears from the ecosystem may weaken the survival chances of another. The loss of a keystone species—an organism that links many other species together—much like the center keystone of an arch—could cause a significant disruption in the biological chain of the entire system. For example, keystone specie in the Amazon rainforest is the *agouti,* a ground dwelling rodent, which the Brazil nuttree *Berthelletia excelsa* depend upon for its survival. The agouti feeds exclusively on Brazil nut seeds. It is the only animal with teeth strong enough to open the nut seed pods. While the agouti feeds on the Brazil nut seeds, it also scatters these seeds across the forest by burying caches far away from the parent tree. As the young nut tree is growing, it depends on the Amazon *Euglossine* orchid bee. Without the bees' pollination, nut reproduction is not possible. No wonder there has been little success growing Brazil nuts on private plantations, for they only grow in primary Amazon rainforest.

Constantine Issighos   *The Amazon Exploration Series*

AMAZONIAN BIRDS AND FLOWERS

Amazon's Nature of Things

The Amazon Exploration Series   *Constantine Issighos*

Amazon's Nature of Things

Constantine Issighos *The Amazon Exploration Series*

24 *Amazon's Nature of Things*

The Amazon Exploration Series   *Constantine Issighos*

Amazon's Nature of Things

The Amazon Exploration Series *Constantine Issighos*

Amazon's Nature of Things 27

The Amazon Exploration Series   *Constantine Issighos*

Amazon's Nature of Things   *29*

The Amazon Exploration Series   *Constantine Issighos*

Indigenous people use blow guns to hunt small animals. The darts are made of palm-leaf midrib and cuffed with cotton.

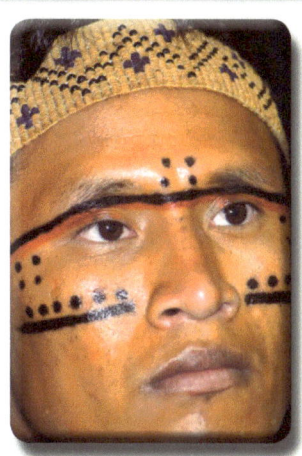

The jaguar people are a reclusive tribe that have little to no outside contact.

The Amazon Exploration Series *Constantine Issighos*

Amazon's Nature of Things

Tribes live in varied environments: in grasslands, in semi-desert or scrubs.

> *Some Brazilian tribes remain fearful and never encounter outsiders.*

> *Those tribes that had contacts with outsiders have been victims of extermination leaving them traumatized.*

> **Global corporations regard the Amazon as just a wild space.**

> **Its resources are free to be used and expropriated and its people neglected.**

The Amazon Exploration Series *Constantine Issighos*

The indigenous people are resisting the threat of massive oil exploration.

Their struggle is for the survival of their livelihood and identity.

Amazon's Nature of Things

For thousands upon thousands of years, the indigenous people of the Amazon have lived in harmony with nature, living off the plants in their environments. Their relationship with nature is beyond intimate, for they are connected in every way. The plants are their friends, for which they have the upmost respect. The flora and fauna provide everything they need.

On my trip into the Upper Amazon rainforest, I encountered a number of medicinal plant gardens. Most of the gardens were stretched over a number of acres, offering several different microclimates for the medicinal and other varieties of plants.

The Incas brought different species from as far away as the interior of the Amazon basin and processed them into medicine.

The Amazon Exploration Series   *Constantine Issighos*

Amazon's Nature of Things

The indigenous people of the Amazon have used plants for ritual healing ceremonies, and in magical religious observances. Some tribes drink tea made from the roots of plants to see the ill spirits of patients. The plant allows them to understand the nature of their ailment and to help the patient. The root-bark of some plants is boiled to produce a brew that is blessed.

When it comes to plants, scientists accept their contribution gradually. In general, scientists have been conducting preliminary tests to determined their toxicity and establish their appropriate dose. For example, since 1970 scientists have been conducting studies, mainly in relation to knee osteoarthritis, to show that the Cat's Claw plant has anti-inflammatory properties.

In the Amazon region, herbal medicine is held in hospitals because common people will only accept herbal medicine.

I had many interesting discussions about the practice of plant medicine, about health and nutritional aids.

The Amazon Exploration Series   *Constantine Issighos*

Amazon's Nature of Things   *47*

www.ingramcontent.com/pod-product-compliance
Lightning Source LLC
Chambersburg PA
CBHW041754040426
42446CB00001B/29